T0402809

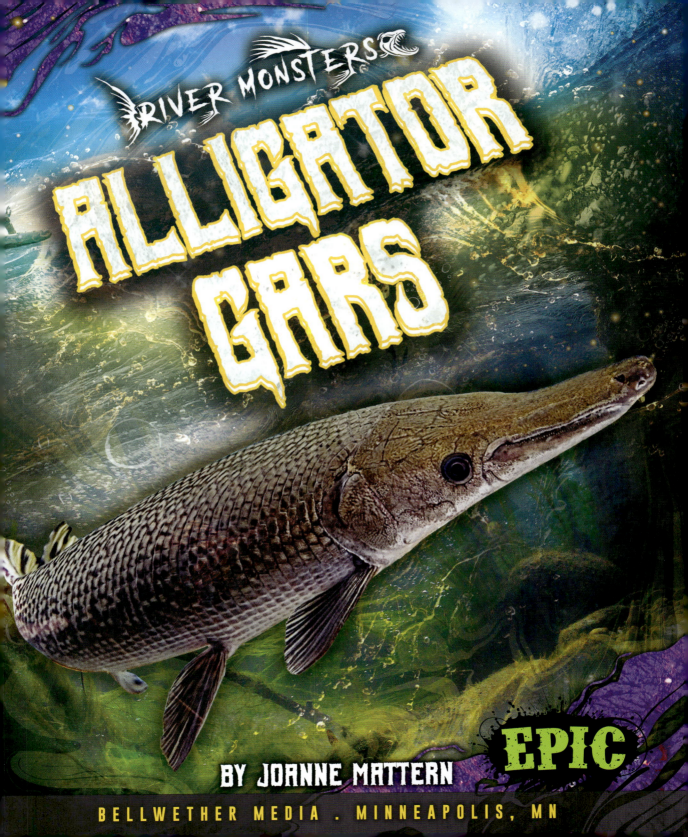

RIVER MONSTERS

ALLIGATOR GARS

BY JOANNE MATTERN

EPIC

BELLWETHER MEDIA . MINNEAPOLIS, MN

EPIC BOOKS are no ordinary books. They burst with intense action, high-speed heroics, and shadows of the unknown. Are you ready for an Epic adventure?

This edition first published in 2024 by Bellwether Media, Inc.

No part of this publication may be reproduced in whole or in part without written permission of the publisher. For information regarding permission, write to Bellwether Media, Inc., Attention: Permissions Department, 6012 Blue Circle Drive, Minnetonka, MN 55343.

Library of Congress Cataloging-in-Publication Data

LC record for Alligator Gars available at: https://lccn.loc.gov/2023039893

Text copyright © 2024 by Bellwether Media, Inc. EPIC and associated logos are trademarks and/or registered trademarks of Bellwether Media, Inc.

Editor: Elizabeth Neuenfeldt   Designer: Josh Brink

Printed in the United States of America, North Mankato, MN.

TABLE OF CONTENTS

ALLIGATOR OR FISH?

Alligator gars are named for their looks. They have similar heads and teeth to alligators!

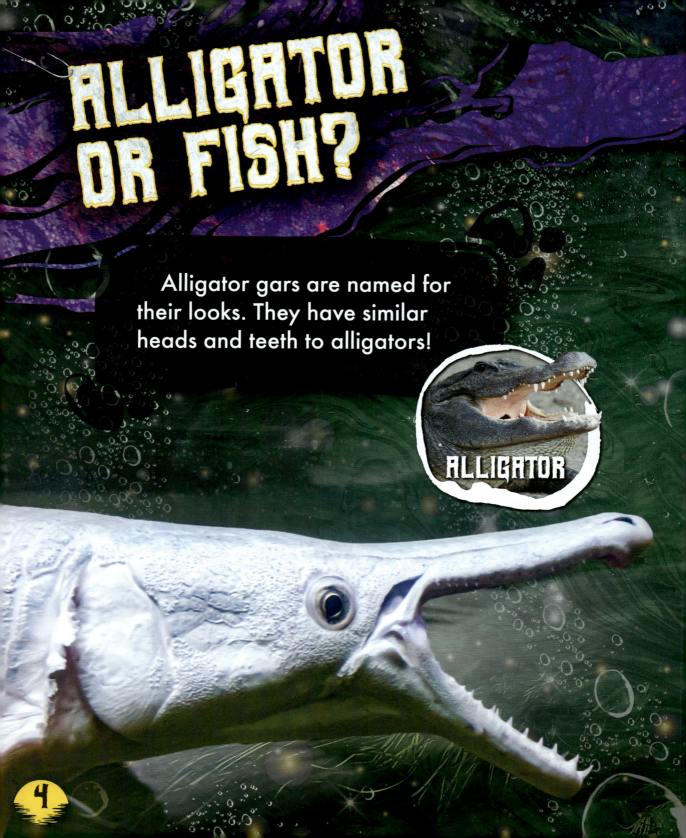

ALLIGATOR

They live in eastern Mexico and the southern United States. They swim in bays, lakes, and rivers.

ALLIGATOR GAR RANGE

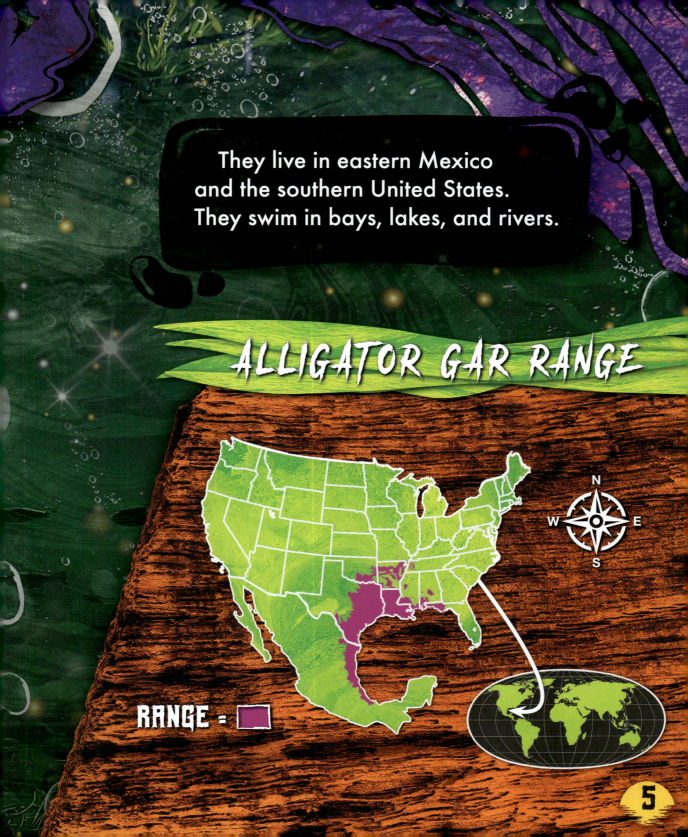

RANGE =

GIANT GARS

Alligator gars are the largest kind of gar. They can be up to 10 feet (3 meters) long. They can weigh a lot, too. Some weigh up to 350 pounds (159 kilograms)!

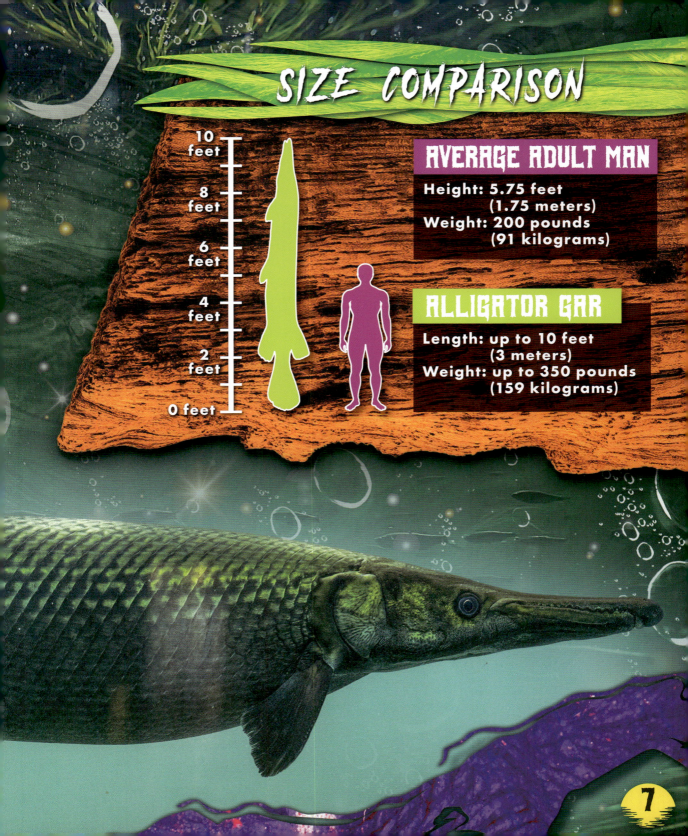

SIZE COMPARISON

10 feet
8 feet
6 feet
4 feet
2 feet
0 feet

AVERAGE ADULT MAN

Height: 5.75 feet
(1.75 meters)
Weight: 200 pounds
(91 kilograms)

ALLIGATOR GAR

Length: up to 10 feet
(3 meters)
Weight: up to 350 pounds
(159 kilograms)

These fish have long, thin bodies. This shape helps them move through water.

Their **snouts** are lined with sharp teeth. Their upper jaws have two rows of teeth!

TEETH ROWS

A LONG-LIVED FISH

Gars have been on Earth for more than 150 million years. They have been around since the time of dinosaurs!

Alligator gars can be gray, green, or brown. Their back fins have dark spots.

FIN

AIR BREATHER

Alligator gars can breathe air! They can live out of the water for a short time.

IDENTIFY AN ALLIGATOR GAR

LONG, THIN BODY

SNOUT

SHARP TEETH

TOUGH SCALES

They are covered with tough **scales**.
These scales are like a suit of armor!
They protect gars from other animals.

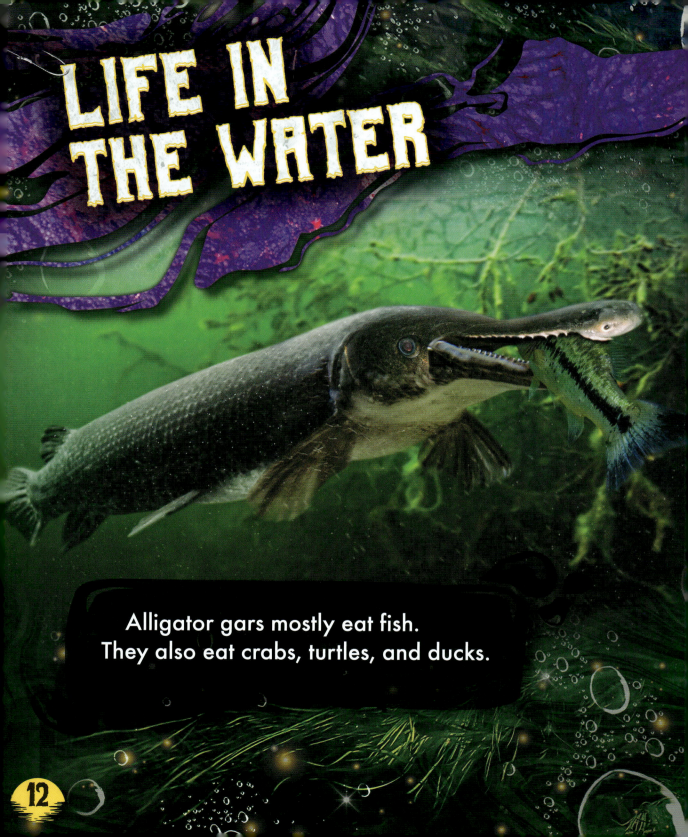

LIFE IN THE WATER

Alligator gars mostly eat fish.
They also eat crabs, turtles, and ducks.

Gars **ambush** their **prey**. They lie still in the water. When prey swims by, gars catch it with their sharp teeth!

RECORD CATCH

0 feet

2 feet

4 feet

6 feet

8 feet

10 feet

WEIGHT
327 pounds
(148 kilograms)

LENGTH
8.4 feet
(2.6 meters)

WHEN WAS IT CAUGHT?
February 14, 2011

WHERE WAS IT CAUGHT?
Chotard Lake, Mississippi

Female alligator gars can lay thousands of eggs! They lay eggs in **shallow** water.

DO NOT EAT!

Alligator gar eggs are poisonous. If other animals eat the eggs, they get very sick!

YOUNG ALLIGATOR GARS

Young gars take care of themselves. They eat **insects** and small fish.

SAVING THE ALLIGATOR GAR

Alligator gars face dangers from people.

For years, people caught as many of them as they could. This led to **overfishing**. Alligator gar numbers have gotten smaller.

CAUGHT ALLIGATOR GAR

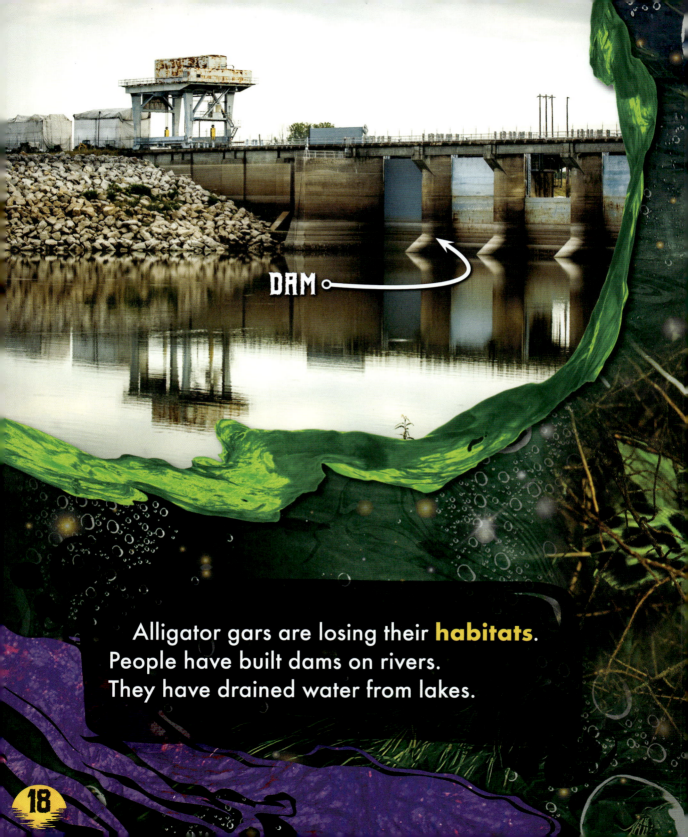

DAM

Alligator gars are losing their **habitats**. People have built dams on rivers. They have drained water from lakes.

These fish have fewer places to swim and lay eggs. Fewer of them can grow up.

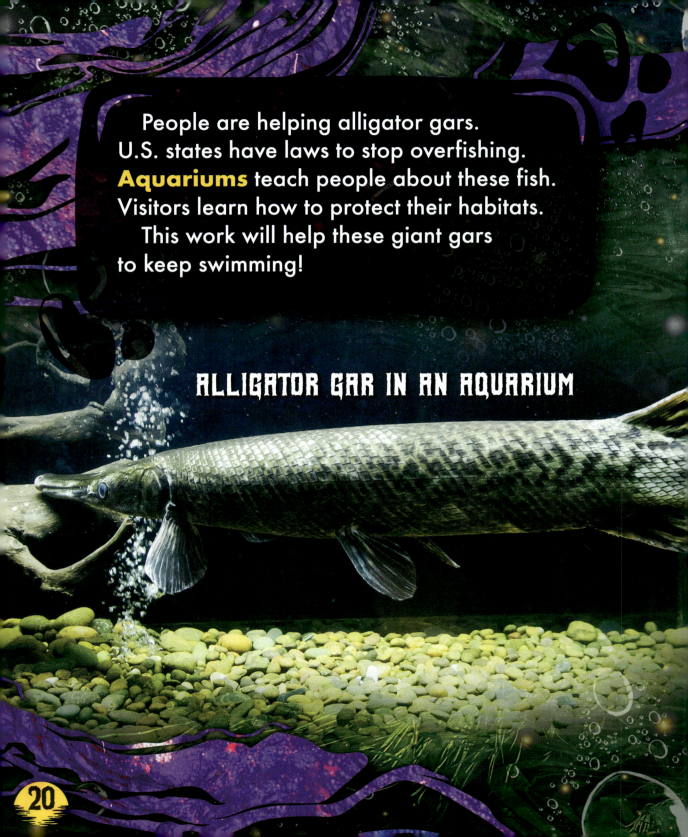

People are helping alligator gars.
U.S. states have laws to stop overfishing.
Aquariums teach people about these fish.
Visitors learn how to protect their habitats.
This work will help these giant gars
to keep swimming!

ALLIGATOR GAR IN AN AQUARIUM

ALLIGATOR GAR STATS

LEAST CONCERN	NEAR THREATENED	VULNERABLE	ENDANGERED	CRITICALLY ENDANGERED	EXTINCT IN THE WILD	EXTINCT

LIFE SPAN
up to 50 years

THREATS
overfishing, habitat loss

GLOSSARY

ambush—to attack by surprise

aquariums—buildings where people can see and learn about fish and other underwater creatures

habitats—places where animals live

insects—small animals with six legs and hard outer bodies; an insect's body is divided into three parts.

overfishing—using up the number of fish by fishing too much

prey—animals that are hunted by other animals for food

scales—small plates that cover the bodies of some fish

shallow—not deep

snouts—the noses and mouths of some animals

TO LEARN MORE

AT THE LIBRARY

Forest, Christopher. *Fish*. Minneapolis, Minn.: Abdo Publishing, 2021.

Green, Sara. *Rivers*. Minneapolis, Minn.: Bellwether Media, 2022.

Mattern, Joanne. *American Paddlefish*. Minneapolis, Minn.: Bellwether Media, 2024.

ON THE WEB

FACTSURFER

Factsurfer.com gives you a safe, fun way to find more information.

1. Go to www.factsurfer.com.

2. Enter "alligator gars" into the search box and click 🔍.

3. Select your book cover to see a list of related content.

INDEX

The images in this book are reproduced through the courtesy of: ProjectManhattan/ Wiki Commons, cover; Rocksweeper, pp. 2-3, 22-23, 24 (background); Elliotte Rusty Harold, p. 4 (alligator); Charlotte Bleijenberg, p. 4 (alligator gar); Khairul Ishra, pp. 6-7; Danny Ye, p. 8; Ryan Hagerty/ USFWS National Digital Library, pp. 9 (teeth rows), 11 (tough scales), 21; NiAk Stock, p. 9; Eugene Sim, p. 10; Wiki Commons, p. 11 (long, thin body); benaung, p. 11 (snout); David Stonner/ AP Newsroom, p. 11 (sharp teeth); Thayut Sutheeravut, pp. 11, 17; Photoshot, p. 12; tunart, pp. 14-15; Rogelio V. Solis/ AP Newsroom, p. 15; Mark Conlin/ AP Newsroom, pp. 16-17; Alison Jones/ Alamy, p. 18; Miropa, pp. 18-19; subinpumsom, p. 20.